# Cellulite
# Revolution

*Also by Leslie Kenton*

THE JOY OF BEAUTY
ULTRAHEALTH
RAW ENERGY (with Susannah Kenton)
RAW ENERGY RECIPES (with Susannah Kenton)
AGELESS AGEING
THE BIOGENIC DIET
10 DAY CLEAN-UP PLAN

# Cellulite
# Revolution

*SIX STEPS TO A NEW BODY ECOLOGY*

## Leslie Kenton

EBURY PRESS · LONDON

First published in 1992 by Ebury Press
an imprint of
The Random Century Group Ltd
Random Century House
20 Vauxhall Bridge Road
London SW1V 2SA

A catalogue record for this book is available from the British Library

ISBN 0 09 177168 4

Filmset in Baskerville by Textype Typesetters, Cambridge
Printed and Bound in Great Britain by Mackays of Chatham plc, Kent.
Chart on page 77 reproduced by kind permission of
Maxine Rogers/*Observer*, based on a chart in *The Biogenic Diet*
by Leslie Kenton (Arrow Books)

**For my mother**

whose beauty was dazzling yet
who could see so little of it herself

The material in this book is intended for informational purposes only. None of the suggestions or information is meant in any way to be prescriptive. Any attempt to treat a medical condition should always come under the direction of a competent physician – preferably one who is familiar with naturopathic techniques and nutrition. I am only a reporter. Yet I am also a woman who has a profound interest in helping myself and others to maximize potentials for positive health. This includes being able to live at a high level of energy, good looks and creativity. For, strange as it may seem to someone schooled only in symptomatic treatment (the 'you've-got-a-headache-you-take-a-pill' mentality), all three are expressions of harmony within a living organic system – expressions of good ecology.

# Contents

## Chapter One
## THE CHALLENGE

# Ecologics

I have little patience with nonsense written about cellulite. The silly debates about whether or not it exists and the trivial yet often painful treatments designed to banish it usually miss the point. Cellulite is no simple cosmetic problem of concern only to vain women who have been sold a bill of goods by the beauty industry. It is a sign that internal pollution is present in parts of your body which can not only reduce your energy levels but mar physical beauty as well. Whether or not you care passionately about having smooth sleek thighs, if you see cellulite developing you can be sure your body is telling you that something within needs attention. Just as the appearance of slime in a river bed indicates that the ecology of the earth is disturbed, a peau d'orange thigh tells a woman that the ecology of her body is out of kilter, and if you want to shed your cellulite nothing short of a revolution in body ecology is called for.

## Meet The Ecology Of The Planet

Ecology is that branch of biology which deals with the relations of living organisms to other organisms and non-living things. It deals with extremely complex interactions, relationships, rhythms, chemical alterations, seasons and processes. Scientists who study the ecology of our planet are also interested in energetics. They examine energy pathways and outputs. They explore how the presence of certain chemicals in the environment or alterations in temperature, or the proliferation of specific life forms either supports or interferes with the life processes of other organisms.

What we have come to realize in the past twenty years is that the health – indeed the *survival* – of our planet depends very much on our doing everything we can to re-establish and maintain good ecology whether or not we are dealing in a small way with, say, a farm or woods, or in a large way with a whole continent. The destruction of the ozone layer in recent years, increasing pollution in the air and water, the depletion of organic matter in the soils and widespread deforestation have now disrupted planetary ecology to a degree that was once unthinkable. They have also set scientists frantically searching for keys for helping to re-establish ecological balance. The necessity of good planetary ecology has been further highlighted recently by a growing acceptance of scientist James Lovelock's Gaia hypothesis. Lovelock suggests that the earth, far from being a mass of dead minerals hurtling through space at great speed, appears to be an almost infinitely complex organic living system – a system of which we ourselves are a part.

## What Is Body Ecology?

Just as the planet has an ecology on which its health depends, so does your body. Its every cell, every vessel, every tissue interacts in highly complex ways either directly or obliquely with every other part. All of your organs and glands and systems not only speak to each other chemically via the metabolic processes which break down nutrients to make them available for cells to use, produce energy for movement and eliminate wastes; they also communicate via subtle energetic pathways. Some of these were charted by Oriental medicine in the treatment of acupuncture and are still used in the application of pressure at specific areas which form the basis of Oriental medicine as well as techniques like shiatsu and reflexology.

The vastly complex living system which is your body has a magnificent ability to regulate itself, taking into account the food you eat, the air you breathe, the stresses you are under, the physical demands made upon you, your age and all the other factors that come into play in your life – provided, of course, it is not overburdened by excess fatigue, stress or pollution and provided its metabolic processes have at their disposal a full complement of the essential nutrients on which they run. This ability of the living body to take in and break down nutrients, to channel them into the specific metabolic processes which maintain life and to eliminate wastes is all part of maintaining its ecology. The problem is that pollution in our air, water and food continues to increase, placing real burdens on the immune system. At the same time the availability of a good balance of essential nutrients in our over-processed foods continues to decline.

One of the many obvious consequences of this decline is the production of cellulite in flesh. When the body's ecology is good then your whole body works well and you have plenty of energy. You don't develop cellulite; neither do you show signs of premature ageing. And, what is most frequently forgotten, you also experience a high level of awareness and autonomy – you find it easier to make your own decisions from a position of mental clarity and physical power.

## A 'Living Revolution'

The name 'Cellulite Revolution' is no idle hyperbole. For, if you are serious about ridding your body of cellulite and keeping it away, nothing short of a revolution is called for – a revolution which involves how you care for yourself, eat, deal with stress and move – a revolution which leads step by step to a whole new body ecology.

This practical little guide offers a six point plan for revolutionizing, rebalancing and re-establishing healthy body ecology to help you live cellulite-free. It includes:

**The Breakdown** – for detoxifying your body, eliminating stasis and dissolving hardened connective tissue.

**The Buildup** – for restructuring new collagen and enhancing metabolic pathways.

**The Energize** – for enlivening, from molecular level right on up to total organism.

**The Smoothout** – for body sculpting from without.

**The Rebalance** – for total body regeneration from within through conscientious food combining.

**The Reclaim** – for reconnecting with the deep ecology of sexuality.

When you support and rebalance your body's ecology at the most profound levels through diet, the use of specific complexes from nature, movement, massage

4

and re-establishing connections with the deepest layers of sexuality, you can not only banish cellulite. You also empower yourself and make it easier to maximize all your potentials. The Cellulite Revolution *begins* with smoother sleeker thighs. But don't be surprised if it takes you a lot further than you have bargained for.

It is my hope that in the process of exploring some of the techniques and tools you will find in the pages that follow, you will experience for yourself just how potent the life force working through your body is – that you will really come to *know* it from within (something which I think women have a particular ability to do). Most important of all, I hope you will come to *trust* it. Then you will discover for yourself that, used wisely, all of the techniques and tools for keeping your flesh cellulite-free are nothing more than ways of aligning yourself to the deepest needs of your body and supporting its own ecology in the best possible way.

The process of getting from here to there is rather like taking a journey – a journey that brings you deeper in touch with the miracle of your living body. It is a journey which offers greater physical beauty, more energy and the expanded awareness which leads to being able to make ever more effective use of your own quite individual brand of creativity. All of these things can be fruits of improved body ecology. In recent years I have come to believe that it is just this kind of energy and creativity that is needed if each of us as women is effectively to make our fullest contribution to the process of caring for the ecology of the living planet.

Chapter Two
THE CHALLENGE

# The Inside Story

Cellulite makes everybody uneasy – from the woman who worries about her orange-peel thighs to the British or American 'obesity expert' intent on proving that fat is fat, cellulite is nothing more than a figment of foolish women's imagination, and what any woman with lumpy thighs should do is get down to a good old calorie-controlled diet to shed it. Even staunch feminists who write hard-hitting polemics about the coercion of women by the beauty industry get het up about cellulite. It is, they insist, something invented by fashion magazines to make women feel bad about themselves. Meanwhile hundreds of thousands of women with the problem bemoan their fate at having contracted a 'non-existent' condition and hope that if only they spend a little more money or endure a little more discomfort from one of the high-tech treat-ments – being pricked with multi-injector syringes or subjected to brutal pummelling for instance – it will make their legs smooth, sleek and svelte.

## Banishing Disbelief

On the desk before me lie medical papers from all over Europe and America on cellulite, its cause and its development as well as proposed solutions to this lumpy bumpy flesh which can mar the thighs of even the leanest women. As of this moment literally hundreds of medical references to cellulite exist, some of them going back a hundred and fifty years. So next time someone tries to tell you that you are imagining peau d'orange thighs smile knowingly and ignore them.

None of the theories, analyses and descriptions of elaborate chemical treatments for cellulite have the full answer. In part this is because cellulite is a difficult condition to study *in vivo* – within the body of a woman who has it – since this means performing a biopsy of the tissue which is a painful medical process. In part it is because cellulite is a many-faceted syndrome with no *single* cause and no *single* effective treatment.

## What Is Cellulite?

A misnomer catch-all word used to describe the orange-peel syndrome, cellulite is a cosmetic defect which results in jodhpur thighs and what is known as the 'mattress phenomenon' – that is pitting, bulging and deformation of the skin on thighs, hips and abdomen (sometimes even arms and shoulders too) when subjected to a 'pinch test'.

In the medical literature cellulite has been called a variety of things from mesenchymal disease to cellulitic dermo-hypodermosis, edemato-fibrosclerotic panniculopathy and, most recently, panniculosis and liposclerosis. A condition which by any other name smells as odious, cellulite is a syndrome with well-defined clinical, histological and histochemical characteristics.

7

What this means in ordinary language is that cellulite looks a certain way when you examine it objectively with your eyes and fingers. Where it is present in a body you will also find that certain measurable bio-chemical and physical changes have taken place in skin, connective tissues and at the deeper layers of the body. By the way, one thing the disbelievers say *is* true: cellulite *does* often occur in an overweight body. If you are overweight, shedding excess ordinary fat will be essential to shedding your cellulite. But cellulite occurs on the thighs and bottoms of very slim women as well. For it is quite different in many ways to ordinary fat.

## A Chequered History

Cellulite has a shady past full of contradiction and confusion. Far from being some new-fangled notion created by glossy women's magazines, cellulite was first described in depth by European physicians at the beginning of the nineteenth century. It is now believed to affect 80 out of every 100 women in Europe and America. In 1816 Balfour first commented on the cutaneous nodule formations which were later named cellulite. In 1929 P. Lageze, a French physician, discovered that cellulite comes in stages: first, tissues in thighs, buttocks, knees, abdomen and upper arms become traps for free serum outside the capillaries. Then fibrous formations develop, which in time turn into the retracted sclerotic connective fibres which create a dimpled orange-peel effect. After Lageze, many researchers proposed numerous theories about the causes of cellulite but none of them could fully agree. Then, in 1966, two Spanish dermatologists confirmed that, while no inflammation of the tissues is present in cellulite, watery fluid does indeed accumulate in the tissue. They also reported that the molecules of subcutaneous connective tissue in cellulite seem to be larger than molecules in the normal connective tissue because they undergo what is called a hyperpolymerization.

In the 1970s a few researchers such as Braun-Falco and Ribuffo came out in favour of the view that cellulite is simple fat. In later years they were to modify their beliefs considerably. Most European researchers grew increasingly convinced that cellulite is a well-defined clinical condition and a physiological entity. 'A defect of the mesenchyme', said Pisani. 'No, a disturbance in the vasomotor reflex and an irritation of the sympathetic nerve fibres leading to a disturbance of normal fat deposits and water logged tissues', argued Merlin. While Binazzi insisted that 'cellulite' should rightly be renamed oedmàto-sclerotic panniculopathy. In 1972 Muller and Nurnberger showed that where cellulite occurs there is also a decrease in the quantity of elastin fibres in the dermis and a rearrangement of the collagen bundles. Then in 1977 Braun-Falco and Scherwitz demonstrated that a dilation of the lymph vessels takes place in cellulite as well as an enlargement of the adipocytes or fat cells. But it was not until the well-respected Italian anatomo-pathologist and molecular biologist Professor Sergio Curri took up the study of cellulite tissue, that the whole of the European medical world began to stand up and take notice. Now considered the leading scientific authority on cellulite in the world, Curri carried out in-depth studies comparing cellulite to normal fat, and established quite conclusively that cellulite is indeed a specific syndrome.

## A Woman's World

To understand cellulite it is important to understand how your flesh is structured. Let's look at the deeper layers first. They are known as subcutaneous tissues. In your thighs these are made up of three layers of fat with two planes of connective tissue and ground substance in between. This brings us to one of the interesting things about cellulite: it is almost always a female complaint. With a very few remarkable exceptions men simply do not get it. In part this is hormonal. A woman's body is rich in female hormones such as oestrogen which encourages the laying down of fat. (For years farmers injected oestrogen-like substances in cattle and chickens to fatten them rapidly for market.) This is also why cellulite tends first to appear during times of intense hormonal change such as puberty, pregnancy or when a woman goes on a birth control pill. In part, however, cellulite is a woman's condition because the basic construction of subcutaneous tissue of the thigh differs in men and women.

In women the topmost subcutaneous layer is made up of what are termed large 'standing fat-cell chambers' which are separated by radial and arching dividing walls of connective tissue attached to the overlying tissue of the dermis or true skin. The uppermost part of the subcutaneous tissue of men is different. It is thinner and there is a network of criss-crossing connective tissue walls which makes it harder for a man's body to lay down large fat cells and to trap stored wastes and water in the tissues. Also the corium – the connective tissue structure between the true skin and the deeper layers or hypodermis – is thicker in men than in women. You can check on these differences yourself by carrying out a 'pinch test'. It is only pinching the thighs of women that results in the 'mattress phenomenon' with its pitting, bulging and deformation of skin. Pinch the thighs of most men and you will get gentle skin folds or furrows completely without bulges or pits.

## Beware The Ravages Of Time

Age-related changes in women also encourage the buildup of cellulite. For instance, as women get older, their skin gets progressively looser and thinner. This encourages the migration of fat cells into this layer. The connective tissue walls between the chambers of fat cells also get thinner allowing the fat-cell chambers to enlarge – a condition known as hypertrophy. This progressive thinning of connective tissue structures is another major factor in the development of cellulite and creates the granular texture and buckshot feel of much cellulite-riddled flesh.

An examination of cellulite tissue under the microscope also reveals that a number of histological changes have taken place. They include a distension of the lymphatic vessels of the upper skin, for instance, and a decrease in the number of elastic fibres. The circulation of blood, too, has been slowed and the connective fibres have undergone a sclerotic hardening so that the fluids and the wastes they contain become trapped in an unpleasant network which pinches nerve endings (hence the pain in well-developed cellulite) and creates stasis in the tissue – rather like a polluted swamp where energy exchange is reduced. The whole area takes on a deadened quality – a sure sign of poor body ecology.

## A Hard Look At Soft Fat

Curri examined fragments of adipose (fat) tissue taken from the outer thighs of young subjects, obese adults and older subjects and then compared their physical and biochemical structures with those from women with cellulite. Examining cellulite tissue under a microscope and analyzing it chemically using gas chromatography, Curri established conclusively both from a morphological point of view and from a biochemical one that cellulite tissue differs in many ways from normal fat tissue.

Structurally or morphologically, only in cellulite is there:

- a leakage of plasma through weakened capillary walls into the spaces between your fat cells.

- a thickening of connective fibre which encapsulates your fat cells.

- the formation of nodules caused by the hardening of collagen.

- a stretching of your capillaries and blood stagnation with poor circulation.

Biochemically in cellulite there are significant differences in the ratio of certain fatty acids and triglycerides compared to ordinary fatty tissue. These include:

- an increase in stearic acid over palmitic acid.

- an increase in stearic acid over oleic-linoleic acid.

- an increase in unsaturated fatty acids over saturated fatty acids.

## The Four Stages Of Cellulite

In simple terms Curri's findings showed that the structure of cellulite tissue differs considerably in structure and chemical composition from normal fat. It also tends to develop in stages:

**Normal Flesh** – Skin on your thighs and buttocks is smooth when you are standing or lying down. When pinched it folds and furrows but does not pit or bulge. This is the normal skin of most lean and very healthy men and women.

**Stage 1** – Your skin is still smooth when you are standing or lying down but a pinch test reveals the mattress phenomenon of bulging and pitting. Some deformation of the skin surface has taken place. There are signs of waterlogging – interstitial oedema, structural dissociation and the beginnings of tissue dystrophy. Your skin has begun to look pasty. Tissue examination reveals the development of hard fibres in connective tissue.

**Stage 2** – Your skin is smooth when you are lying down but when standing it shows signs of pitting and bulging. (This is common in women who are overweight or past the age of 35). Deep palpitation of your skin produces a dull pain. You cannot detect specific nodules to the touch but micronodules will be seen in tissue examination.

**Stage 3** – The mattress phenomenon is apparent whether you are sitting or lying down. Your flesh is painful – sometimes even when not touched – and macronodules or what is known as hypodermic plaque will be seen whether or not there is a lot of oedema or water retention present. Histological examination will show that nodules are encapsulated in hardened or sclerotic connective tissue. This stage is very common after menopause or when a woman is seriously overweight.

So much for the scientific low down on cellulite, all of which is useful to fall back on next time somebody tries to tell you those lumps and bumps that you worry about are all in your mind or suggest they will disappear in a jiffy on a 900 calorie diet. But the important question for any woman with lumpy flesh is, 'What am I going to do about it?' That is where a total shift in body ecology comes in. And I mean *total*. You can spend as much money as you like and go through as much agony as you like being stuck and prodded and wrapped in special packages but unless you go the whole body approach you will be wasting your money. **Cellulite Revolution** starts with **The Breakdown** – a detoxification plan as the first step towards a new body ecology. It can prepare the way for an easy-to-follow way of eating that can minimize the buildup of wastes in your cells and help rebalance body ecology as long as you continue to follow it.

## Chapter Three
## THE BREAKDOWN

# Waist Disposal

'Excess fat is nothing less than a poison depot in an over-acid organism.' These words were uttered half a century ago by Danish physician Kristine Nolfi – an expert in healing the body through diet. They lie at the core of the cellulite phenomenon. One of your body's most effective ecological mechanisms for protecting itself from excessive poisons taken in through food, air and water or produced from within as a by-product of metabolism is to lock these toxic materials into fat cells. In the case of cellulite this natural protective mechanism goes one stage further – encasing these wastes in the interstitial fluids and ground substance by binding them within hardened connective tissue. There they sit year after year producing jodhpur thighs.

## Personal Energy Crisis

This whole self-protective process is perfectly normal and, all in all, functions rather well, except for two things. First, in the presence of a high level of female hormones it tends to turn into cellulite. Second, it tends to deplete your energy – not only on a cellular level so metabolic processes don't function in an optimal way but overall so you are prone to fatigue and need stimulants such as coffee to get you going and to keep you going. For in any body which has a high level of waste stored in its cells, much of the available energy is channelled into trying to cope with these wastes instead of being used to keep metabolic processes functioning at a high level of efficiency. In broad terms you sense a lack of overall vitality and over the years develop a tendency to become chronically tired – sometimes so much so that it can even become very difficult to make the effort to help yourself. To shed cellulite you need first to help your body detoxify itself and eliminate the pockets of static tissues where, like stagnant ponds in a meadow, toxicity has been allowed to accumulate.

A lot has been written in recent years about detoxification. Some of it can sound quite mystifying. But the whole process is really quite simple. The reason you have built up these pockets of wastes is simply that your body is continually having to cope with more poisons than it can eliminate in the normal day-to-day course of events. Remove some of the burden of what is creating this excess toxicity in your system by laying aside coffee, alcohol and over-processed foods complete with chemical additives for a time, and you are halfway there. Add to that a very simple and *temporary* regime designed to trigger rapid detoxification, some movement (see Chapter 6) and some external help, and quite naturally you trigger your body's own mechanisms for clearing out the junk. This is the first step in the Cellulite Revolution. There are lots of ways you can do it but the simplest of all to begin with is to go on a two-or-three-day applefast.

## Applemagic

The apple has long been valued as health tonic, medicine, cosmetic and bowel-regulator all in one. Apples are low in acidity to help balance stored bodily wastes which tend to be acidic. They stimulate the flow of saliva in the mouth and clear away debris from the teeth. Eating raw fresh apples stimulates circulation in the gums too. In folk medicine the apple was traditionally used for eliminating obesity (in part no doubt because of its detoxifying ability) as well as for the treatment of skin problems, bladder inflammation, anaemia, insomnia, intestinal parasites and even bad breath. In recent years we have come to appreciate the kind of fibre apples contain. In addition to cellulose (the most common variety of fibre such as that in bran which binds water and increases faecal bulk), apples are also rich in pectin – a special form of fibre with exceptional detoxification properties. Unlike cellulose, pectin does *not* bind water. It is *water-soluble*. Pectin has no influence on faecal bulking, but it can be an excellent substance to help lower cholesterol and for eliminating bile acids from the intestines. Also, and in many ways most important of all for keeping cellulite away, pectin is a natural chelating agent for binding dangerous heavy metals in the body such as aluminium, cadmium, mercury and lead, and eliminating them.

## Beware The Heavy Metals

Whether or not you go for music of the same name, heavy metals in your body are something you want to get rid of. These elements, the concentration of which has increased dramatically in our air, foods and water since the Industrial Revolution, can seriously interfere with your body's metabolic functioning and thus challenge its wellbeing. Mercury tends to suppress the levels of white blood cells involved in the immune response. Cadmium displaces the essential element zinc needed for a great many of your body's enzyme systems and renders them inefficient and even inactive (including those that build new collagen and elastin for skin and connective tissues). In the West we now have a concentration of lead in our bodies some 500 to 1,000 times that of our pre-technological ancestors. High levels of this heavy metal age us prematurely, interfere with our mental processes, suppress immunity and contribute to depression. Aluminium, another heavy metal, detrimentally affects the central nervous system. It has recently been associated with the development of pre-senile dementia or Alzheimer's disease.

The presence of all of these elements in excessive quantities (and their concentrations in the human body appear to be increasing with each passing decade) generally interferes with the metabolic processes on which good body ecology and therefore the absence of cellulite depends. It is important to do everything you can to eliminate them from your body. (The alginates, forms of fibre found in seaweeds, also chelate heavy metals and adding sea plants to your diet on an ongoing basis is a good idea, after your applefast is finished.) You also need to be aware of ways you can protect yourself from allowing heavy metals to build up in the first place. Here are a few suggestions:

- Steer clear of tobacco smoke and exhaust fumes

- Don't buy fruit or vegetables from shops in the street where they have been exposed to leaded exhaust fumes

- Don't cook in aluminium pans

- Eat plenty of fibre and nutrient-rich vegetables and fruits.

## More Than An Apple A Day

Now let's get down to the programme. An applefast can be done by any healthy person provided of course your doctor agrees. It was taught to me twenty years ago by Dr Gordon Latto, a British medical doctor who uses nothing but food and breathing and a few herbs to heal even the most complex and chronic conditions. He is almost 80 and one of the most remarkably healthy and vital men I have ever met. The applefast lasts for two or three days (never more, except under doctor's supervision). You eat only raw apples – as many varieties as you want – for breakfast, lunch and dinner as well as in between. Eat all you want, but chew well and always crunch up the seeds too. They contain valuable nutrients that help the process.

During the applefast you need to give up all tea and coffee although you may have as much mineral water or herb tea made with mineral water as you please, sweetened with a little honey if you prefer. The best herb tea of all for **The Breakdown** is solidago or golden rod which you can get from a good herbalist. Like nettle, it has natural diuretic properties to help shift some of the stored water in your tissues but, unlike nettle, it actually tastes *pleasant*.

Don't be surprised if you suffer the odd headache during this dynamic two or three days clear out. (Especially if you have been a dyed-in-the-wool coffee or tea drinker.) This is a sign that the whole process is happening rapidly. If you do, then take a 20-minute epsom salts bath and lie down in a darkened room to rest for 15 minutes afterwards. (More about this in a moment.)

External work on your body is important too to trigger the detoxification process. Start now to incorporate skin brushing into your daily routine. After the applefast is over continue doing it but begin to use other techniques as well to enhance lymphatic drainage (see Chapter 7), to help break up hardened connective tissue, and to keep the detoxification process going while you are rebuilding new, strong connective tissue and ground substance.

## Go To Work On A Thigh

Skin brushing, once looked upon as an occupation of a few eccentrics who liked suffering, is now frequently recommended by health practitioners because of its ability to encourage lymphatic drainage and spring clean your body. It is your lymph system which is largely responsible for clearing your tissues of toxicity and eliminating cellular waste. Lymph drainage is often severely impeded in a cellulite-riddled body.

Spend five minutes a day before your shower or bath brushing your skin with a natural-fibre brush. Begin at the tips of your shoulders and cover your whole body (except the head) with long smooth strokes over shoulders, arms and trunk in a downwards motion, then upwards over your feet, legs and hips. You need only go over your skin once or twice for it to work. How firmly you press depends on how toned your flesh is now. Go easy to begin with. Your skin will soon become fitter and then you will be able to work far more vigorously. This will encourage better circulation, bring energy into 'deadened' areas of flesh, smooth and soften skin and encourage better lymphatic drainage in cellulite-prone areas of your body. You will also release a lot of toxicity through the skin's surface.

You can check for yourself just how efficiently your skin can eliminate wastes by performing a practical experiment with the help of a wet flannel rung out. Every day after you skin brush, take the damp flannel and rub it all over your body. Hang it up and repeat the process with the same flannel the next day. After a few days, the smell of the flannel will be quite revolting because of the large quantity of waste products you have eliminated through your skin's surface. Just think of how much better off you are without them!

## The Cactus Connection

Another powerful adjunct to **The Breakdown** is drinking the biogenic – life generating – juice of the aloe vera plant. Aloe vera is a beautiful cactus – probably the most widely used plant for beauty and healing in the world with a history going back 5,000 years. In every culture which has discovered the aloe vera plant it has been used internally to help digestive problems including peptic and duodenal ulcers, arthritis, rheumatism, constipation, varicose veins and throat, nose and chest infections. Externally it has been used to treat itching, inflammation and bruising, sunburns, burns and eczema, dandruff, insect bites, cuts and injuries.

In an attempt to discover the healing principles of aloe, the plant has been analyzed to show the specific nutritional factors it contains – alkaloids, saponins, fatty acids, glycoproteins, vitamins, minerals, amino acids and other small molecules. None of these things in isolation appear to be of great benefit, but together in the special synergy that exists in the aloe vera plant itself, they do wonderful things for the body – especially in helping eliminate cellulite and keeping it away. Used externally, you will find nothing better than pure aloe vera juice as a base for your own anti-cellulite treatment (see page 61). Used internally it appears to help detoxify the body in general, enhance digestion so that wastes do not build up in the system, improve the quality of micro-organisms in the large intestine which help protect immunity and keep the body clean (all vital factors in the establishment of good body ecology). But it is useful against cellulite in other ways as well, thanks to its being rich in *proteolytic* enzymes.

Proteolytic means protein-digesting. These are the enzymes which help break down protein foods into peptides and free form amino acids for your body to use to rebuild muscle tissue, make enzymes on which the breakdown of fat and the production of energy depend, and manufacture hormones. For many years it was assumed that enzymes taken in through foods (which are themselves made largely from proteins) were *denatured* – that is simply broken down in the digestive processes into their component parts to become part of the amino acid pool out of which new protein substances could be built. In recent years however, biochemists have discovered that this is only partly true. A good proportion of enzymes in food are not completely broken down but actually taken through the walls of the gut where they are carried via the bloodstream into the body.

The proteolytic enzymes in aloe vera which are not broken down completely, such as cinnamic acid, may well be responsible for its positive effect both on rheumatic conditions and on the breakdown of necrotic hardened, protein-based connective tissue that is essential to eliminating cellulite. That remains to be proven. In recent years scientists have also discovered that aloe vera juice has bacteriostatic activity and that it enhances the development of capillaries and circulation in general, reduces water retention and inflammation and speeds up cellular reproduction in skin. Yet no one has as yet been able to find the exact pharmacological principle or principles involved in its healing properties. What is known is that in order to make use of aloe vera's healing properties, you either have to use the juice fresh from the cut leaves of a cactus which is at least four years old or it has to be carefully processed at extremely low temperatures to preserve its biogenic properties. Most aloe vera on the market is made from crushed leaves that have been filtered and then pasteurized at 77°C. This produces an inexpensive but bitter and largely useless product. Good aloe vera is hard to come by (see Resources, page 84). It must be kept refrigerated on opening and used within a month.

By whatever method it acts, taking aloe vera juice is enormously useful internally as part of **The Breakdown** and **The Buildup** as well as externally as part of **The Smoothout**. You drink two tablespoons on awakening, between meals and then just before bed. Good aloe vera juice is one of the cleanest and most refreshing tastes you will find anywhere. I like it 'on the rocks' with a twist of lime.

## Salts Of The Earth

It is an old practice and a potent one for eliminating wastes through the surface of the skin to take epsom salts baths. Epsom salts are magnesium sulphate. Both magnesium and sulphate molecules have an ability to leech excess sodium, phosphorous and

23

nitrogenous wastes from the body. This is why athletes use them to relieve muscular pain and why they are wonderful as a way of unwinding during periods of prolonged stress.

Magnesium and sulphur are also some of the most alkalinizing earth minerals. When you get into an epsom salts bath the magnesium sulphur quite literally disperses the pressure in your body and you experience in a very real way a sense of physical and emotional relief and of restored balance. The reduction of toxicity in your body after an epsom salts bath frees energy for more efficient use. But the beneficial effects of epsom salts baths don't end in their ability to detoxify the body chemically. There are some very interesting reasons for the benefits they can bring when you look at how they act on the body from an energetic point of view: magnesium sulphate dissolved in a body of water creates a static, unified, electrical field. Immersing your body in this field helps neutralize excess electrical charges from one area of the body and to creates a magnetic balance. There is nothing quite so good as an epsom salts bath when you have been on a long flight or are suffering from jet lag or emotional tension or upset. During **The Breakdown**, taking an epsom salts bath once a day (preferably just before bed) helps speed the detoxification process and minimize any negative experience such as aches and pains or fatigue or nervousness which sometimes come with eliminating stored wastes rapidly. An epsom salts bath can also be of tremendous help later to keep the cleansing process going – taken, say, once or twice a week. Here's how: take 2 cups of household grade epsom salts (available from the chemist), pour it into the bath and fill the bath with blood-heat water. Then immerse yourself for 20 to 30 minutes, topping up

24

with warm water when necessary to maintain a comfortable temperature. Afterwards, lie down for 15 minutes or, better still, have an epsom salts bath just before you go to bed in the evening.

## Go Easy For A While

Rest is another important part of **The Breakdown**. Good body ecology depends very much on a balance between anabolic and catabolic activities. Anabolic activities are those that build up tissues and repair cells. All of these activities can be carried out successfully if your body's catabolic processes – those involved in breaking down old proteins for instance and in eliminating old wastes – are also working well. In many women with cellulite, the anabolic processes far outstrip the catabolic ones – particularly in the cellulite-prone areas of their body such as the thighs and tummies – so that it would seem that almost everything they do simply builds more and more tissue. Taking time out to rest, read, listen to music, sleep – in short to do all of those things which trigger the parasympathetic branch of your autonomic nervous system – can also set you on the road to shedding unwanted tissue. So plan your applefast for over a weekend and make it three days if you possibly can of gentle rest, relaxation and pleasure. It really is necessary if you are going to make a fundamental shift in your metabolic balance that will begin the process toward a new body ecology to keep you cellulite-free.

# Chapter Four
## THE BUILDUP

# Pure Metabolics

What many advocates of detoxification forget is that in clearing cellulite it is not enough only to clear out your body, shifting wastes and excessive water out of tissues and encouraging the breakdown of whatever hardened connective tissue is present. You also need to help the tissues rebuild themselves in a healthier, sleeker form. This means rebuilding the metabolic machinery on which good body ecology, good looks and resistance to premature ageing depend. That's where **The Buildup** comes in. It is all about replenishing, refurbishing, helping your body to regenerate so that old worn-out tissue is replaced, renewed and restored. Again it is your body that will do the work. But it is your job to see that you supply it with everything it needs to do so.

## Patterns Of Evolution

Our bodies have developed throughout evolution via multiple interactions to make use of numerous substances that occur in nature – from minerals like iodine, chromium, selenium and calcium to the vitamins and elements such as nitrogen and sulphur as well as a myriad of other less-understood substances of plant origin – from the flavonoids to the tannins. Biochemists now do understand that there is *never* a deficiency of only one substance – say a vitamin or mineral alone. Neither does any vitamin or mineral act in the body all by itself.

The whole foundation of the biological functioning of nutrients in the various metabolic processes in which they are involved depends upon their *synergy* – their multiple interactions within your body. And for these functions to be carried out properly, nutritional substances need to be supplied to it in pretty much the same balance and concentrations that they occur in nature when you eat unprocessed foods grown in healthy soils. For it was just these foods throughout millions of years of evolution that served to develop the precise mechanisms by which the body looks after life and health.

This part of the Cellulite Revolution, **The Buildup**, is all about supplying your body with the best complement of all it needs to refurbish, rebuild, renew itself. These days, with the challenge of increasing pollution, depletion of essential nutrients in poorly grown and over-processed foods, and lifestyles that sometimes don't serve the demands of health at the highest levels, this is no mean task.

## The Myth Of The Well-Balanced Diet

You have heard it all before. So long as you eat a 'well-balanced diet' you have no problem getting all the vitamins, minerals, essential fatty acids and so forth that you need for health and beauty. Right? Wrong.

Large-scale studies carried out on people living on a Western diet done even as long as 25 years ago show that the so-called well-balanced diet no longer exists. The Health and Nutrition Examination Survey in America was one of the biggest. It looked at 20,000 people from age one to seventy-four, what they ate, the levels of nutrients in their blood and any signs of nutritional deficiencies. Even using very conservative levels as the norm, it found huge dietary deficiencies. For example 9 out of 10 women were low in iron. Half of the women tested had insufficient calcium. More than 60 per cent of the men and women studied showed at least one symptom of malnutrition regardless of income level. Since then, thanks to ever-increasing levels of pesticides and chemical flavourings and colourings in our foods (all of which tend to unbalance the body's metabolic processes and deplete it of the nutrients it needs to maintain good body ecology), matters have become much worse. It is helpful to remember all this next time you hear another facile suggestion that you should not concern yourself about whether or not you have a good balance of nutrients to support high-level health so long as you are getting those good old meat-and-two-veg meals every day.

Unless you live in the country, grow all your own foods organically and take great care with everything you eat, chances are you are going to need some extra support for all the metabolic processes concerned with building new connective tissue and to help you re-establish the good body ecology that can keep you cellulite-free in the future.

## The Vitamin Dilemma

Does this mean taking lots of vitamins and mineral supplements? It can. There are some very good ones on the market although there are some very poor ones too. Two things determine whether or not a vitamin or mineral supplement is good. The first is the balance between various nutrients. Most vitamin and mineral supplements are put together using more of the cheaper vitamins and less of the more expensive ones. Taking such a supplement over a period of time can seriously imbalance your system. The second factor in determining whether or not a vitamin and mineral supplement is good is how *bio-available* are the vitamins and minerals it contains.

Bio-availability is the measure of how much of a specific nutrient your body is able to make use of. For instance, there are many forms of minerals on the market which you can take in massive quantities yet be able to use only a fraction of the nutrient they contain. Take zinc for instance. The most common form of this mineral is zinc gluconate. It is very inexpensive to produce which is why zinc gluconate is so common in nutritional supplements. The trouble is that zinc gluconate is not very bio-available. To get a form of zinc which your body can use you need to go for something like zinc citrate or, even better, zinc picolinate although both are massively more expensive to produce and therefore much more expensive to buy.

## Metabolic Helpers And Purifiers

In many ways far more useful than even the best of the man-made vitamin and mineral supplements are the rich combinations of nutrients found in nature in certain plants. For no matter how skilled the formulators of nutritional supplements become they will still never be able to produce products which have the synergistic power of these complexes – complexes which, although much lower in the quantities of minerals, vitamins and other essential substances than man-made pills, are highly bio-available and superbly balanced for perfect synergy so that each substance beautifully complements and emphasizes the actions of others in your body.

When it comes to re-establishing good body ecology there is nothing to beat using some of these remarkable complexes. This is very much the direction that twenty-first century nutritional medicine is beginning to take. What plants specifically? The aloe vera cactus, carefully processed horsetail silica, fresh raw vegetables and fruits (preferably home grown organically), the single-celled green algae spirulina and certain sea plants which are rich in minerals in a balance very close to that of tissues and fluids in your body. Such things can offer potent help in banishing cellulite and keeping it away.

## Silica – Not Only For Computers

Let's look at silica first. The second most widely available element on the planet, silica in its *organic* form is an element essential to human health and life. Silica never exists in isolation but always in compounds and it has the remarkable ability to form long complex molecules with powerful bonds – molecules which are tremendously strong and stable. That is why structurally strong tissues in your body such as skin, collagen, connective tissue, arteries, and tendons as well as the cornea of the eye all contain large quantities of silica. So do the enamel of your teeth, your nails, your hair, and many important glands such as the adrenals, thymus, pancreas and spleen.

Silica plays an essential role in the development and maintenance of cellulite-free flesh. When there is an adequate supply in your body this brings a high level of support to the metabolic pathways responsible for the production of strong new collagen, elastin and ground substance in skin. If your metabolic processes do not have an optimal supply of silica at their disposal, this and this alone (quite apart from any other sub-clinical deficiencies of minerals or trace elements which might be present), can severely impede the rebuilding of good connective tissue and skin and contribute to lumpy, sagging flesh. To give you some idea of just how potent an effect organic silica supplementation can have, when it has been given *in vitro* to cell cultures, they increase their collagen production by an amazing 243 per cent.

A woman's daily requirement of silica is rather high at 20-30 mg. Because the element is so widespread in nature it was long assumed that we would get all we need from our foods. Organic matter in the soils should by rights break down the inorganic silica in the earth and render it available to us in its organic, bio-available form through the foods we eat. The trouble is that high-tech farming in the past 50 years has destroyed much organic matter in our soils so that our fruits and vegetables, once rich in organic silica, are now depleted of it.

Also, modern food processing tends to remove much of the little that remains so that many women are not receiving optimal quantities of this precious nutrient. The Western diet rich in white flour, white rice, peeled vegetables, tinned, frozen or highly processed foods tends to be very low in organic silica.

# Right From The Horse's Tail

There is only one extremely rich source known to man of this precious yet much neglected nutrient: horsetail – the beautiful and primitive *equisetum arvense* – one of the world's earliest forms of plant life.

This curious little perennial, which grows in forests, meadows and marshlands, has long been used by folk healers to treat numerous ailments from rheumatism and tonsillitis to wound healing. The horsetail plant has a remarkable structure with two types of aerial stalks, one of which is fertile and looks after the plant's reproduction and the other which is sterile. It is the sterile stalk which can be harvested to produce organic silica supplements. For here is found the element silica bound together with 10 other trace elements plus flavonoids, phenolic acids, organic acids and plant sterols in superb synergy – all of which contribute to a remarkable health-supporting complex.

# Silica Par Excellence

A French biochemist Professor Louis Kervran began in 1949 to study the effects of trace elements on living organisms and became fascinated with silica's health-enhancing effects on the human body. Kervran was aware that many people in the West, unbeknown to them, have sub-clinical deficiencies of silica because of our depleted soils and highly processed foods. He also knew that a good supply of organic silica in the form of a nutritional supplement was hard to come by and that taking unprocessed silica direct from the horsetail plant as a ground-up herb can lead to gastric irritation.

Kervran worked for several years to develop a revolutionary technique of deriving a *natural* silica extract using no chemicals or solvents that would respect the integrity of the wonderful complex of nutrients and plant substances which are bound together with the organic silica in horsetail. The result is a plant-derived supplement with a remarkable ability to support the body's metabolic processes involved in rebuilding the collagen of connective tissue, the ground substance in which it sits and which can even assist your body in dealing better with stress. One more bonus: because of its ability to bind and keep minerals in living tissue and to strengthen the keratin bonds, supplemental organic silica often improves the strength and beauty of hair and nails better than anything I have ever come across.

As you get older the amount of silica present in your body decreases year by year. With the decrease comes increasing weakness and fragility of hair, nails, connective tissue, veins, the ground substance of skin and arteries. A major part of **The Buildup** is replacing old weakened and disordered connective tissue as well as producing new, clean and clear ground substance to take its place so that wastes are no longer trapped in peau d'orange pockets on hips and thighs and elsewhere in your body, which also helps protect all tissue from cellulite forming in the future. Most women notice a difference within 3 to 6 weeks of beginning to take between 2 and 6 tablets a day with meals. Improvement in hair and nails tends to occur at about the same rate.

Two final words about organic silica. First, a major factor in the formation of peau d'orange in your body is the buildup of excessive wastes which your body produces as a by-product of excessive stress. Silica is in particularly high concentration in three glands in your body – the spleen, the adrenals and the thymus (which is particularly important in keeping immunity high). Many people who supplement their diet with natural organic silica report an enhancement in their ability to handle stress even over long periods without difficulty. Being able to do that is of tremendous help in getting rid of cellulite and keeping it away. If you decide to make organic silica part of your own personal anti-cellulite programme, make sure the kind you buy has been processed without chemicals and is highly bio-available – which means in a form your body can easily make use of (see Resources, page 85). You should never take powdered horsetail herb, incidentally, for it is extremely irritating to the intestines besides which your body will be able to make very little use of the silica present since very little of it will be bio-available.

## Plants From The Depths

Another source of plant complexes particularly useful in banishing cellulite and re-establishing good body ecology is the sea. All seaweeds – from kelp to dulse, to the Japanese foods like nori and kombu – are rich in the minerals which your body's metabolic processes require to function properly. In a time when our foods are becoming increasingly depleted in important minerals and trace elements the use of plants from the sea becomes more and more important. Even things which your system requires in minute quantities such as vanadium, chromium and lithium are found in sea plants.

Sea plants also tend to be rich in special forms of fibre called the alginates which have the ability to bind and remove heavy metals from the body. And they are rich in organic iodine (see page 70) which, used both internally and externally, tends to stimulate metabolic processes. A good supplement of sea plants which have been collected from unpolluted waters and then 'atomized' or broken into very fine particles can offer another source of important metabolic support on any anti-cellulite regime. This process of atomization is very important in choosing any supplement based on sea plants. For seaweeds tend to have very hard cell walls and, unless these plants are extracted or their cell walls are exploded to make their mineral contents more easy for the body to absorb, much of the metabolic treasures they contain remain hardly available to the body. When choosing a good supplement of sea plants it is also important to make sure their source is unpolluted waters. Like fish that live in chemically contaminated waters, these plants can absorb many negative elements which can badly disturb body ecology and which you certainly do not want in your body.

## Second Stage Aloe

The aloe vera plant helps in the detoxification process which is why it plays such an important part in **The Breakdown**. It can offer tremendous support in **The Buildup**, too, but in totally different ways. Good body ecology depends on an adequate supply of essential elements and nutrients as well as the ability of your digestive system to absorb these nutrients with maximum efficiency while *not* absorbing wastes and poisons through the wall of the gut into the blood stream. The body's ability to do this can be impeded by poor digestion, by the proliferation of micro-organisms such as candida albicans in the digestive tract or a heavy overgrowth of negative bacteria in the intestines which do not benefit the body. So your system is constantly carrying a burden which for the sake of cellulite-free flesh, protection against illness and premature ageing, as well as keeping energy levels high, you want to get rid of. Aloe vera can help here too. It calms the stomach and supports efficient, easy digestion. It also enhances gastric motility so that wastes are more efficiently eliminated from the body, and improves the quality of micro-organisms in the organs of digestion and elimination. Aloe vera even helps in the digestion and assimilation of proteins and calms the kind of food sensitivities where a woman who reaches for a biscuit to go with a cup of tea finds herself eating the whole packet.

During **The Buildup** period it can often be helpful to take a small glass of pure low-heat processed aloe vera juice on rising, between breakfast and lunch and lunch and dinner as well as just before you go to bed. Aloe vera makes a delicious drink and, like silica and sea plants, can play a central role in re-establishing the kind of body ecology that keeps your flesh cellulite-free. All three are also useful in helping to slim down your body if in addition to cellulite you need to shed ordinary fat.

Chapter Five

THE BUILDUP

# Power Flesh

Many women with cellulite go on and off slimming diets where they lose weight rapidly and then regain it only to lose some more in a cyclic pattern year after year. More than practically anything else this encourages the buildup of cellulite in the body. Crash dieting is the worst thing you can do if you want to get rid of cellulite. For eating programmes which severely restrict calorie intake result in your losing large quantities of water, electrolytes, minerals, glycogen stores and other fat-free tissue including muscle with only minimal loss of fat from your body.

## Beware Slimming Sludge

Crash dieting depletes your body of its supply of nutrients necessary to fuel the exact metabolic processes on which the elimination of cellulite depends. It also breaks down the muscle tissue in your body on which firm flesh depends and gradually replaces it with fat and sludge which turns into more cellulite. In the process you can experience disturbances in blood-sugar regulating mechanisms so you suffer periods of fatigue during the day and then have to fight with so-called 'will power' to keep from eating biscuits and chocolate and coffee just to keep going (all of which further pollute your body, deplete your energy reserves and contribute to the buildup of yet more tissue sludge and cellulite).

If losing fat needs to be part of your own anti-cellulite programme stay away from slimming programmes that severely restrict calories. Instead, get into a dynamic exercise programme (see Chapter 6) and make sure you supply your body with the full complement of nutrients it needs to rebuild itself by using good food supplements. What is a desirable weight-loss programme? It is one which is nutritionally sound, only restricts your calorie intake by around 500 to 800 calories and which therefore results in *gradual* weight loss of no more than one kilo or a couple of pounds a week. In that way, while you are shedding fat you will be building strong, sleek, firm muscles to replace the pockets of tissue sludge and cellulite. This is what I call power flesh.

## Proteins For Power Flesh

Creating power flesh, that is banishing flab and rebuilding your body in firm sleek contours, takes time. And it can't be done without good protein. Proteins are made of long chains of amino acids – the primary structural components of your body. These amino acids act as building blocks for new muscle which is made up of protein and water. Amino acids also stimulate metabolic processes and hormonal activity and they are key elements in mobilizing fat and cellulite. In fact amino acids are needed for just about every physical process in your body from the production of new hormones to replacement of old tissue with new.

Within your body old proteins are continually being broken down by enzymes into their component amino acids and then reshaped by enzymes into new compounds. Even enzymes themselves are made out of amino acids. Radioisotope tracings have demonstrated that more than 98 per cent of the molecules in your body will be replaced during the next year – your muscles, your blood, your enzymes, even your genes will be made anew. How good they will be depends almost entirely on the raw materials you give your body to work with – what you eat. A biscuit and tea diet will result in a biscuit and tea body, not in power flesh.

To rebuild a strong sleek firm body you need the highest quality proteins. How much is easy to calculate. On any anti-cellulite programme – particularly one on which you are shedding fat – you will need the same quantity of protein that an active woman requires to sustain her body weight if you are exercising, say, an hour a day: This is approximately 1.4 grammes of amino acids per kilogram of body weight (2.2lb). In other words, if you weigh 8½ stone you will need about 76 grammes of protein a day. Once your rebuilding programme is complete, unless you exercise a great deal, you can reduce that requirement to between 0.8 grammes and 1 gramme per kilo of body weight. Unless you supply this quantity of protein foods with a good balance of amino acids, you are asking your body to rebuild itself without giving it the wherewithal to do so – rather like expecting a plant to grow without sunlight and water. And it may surprise you to find that during **The Buildup** you will be eating more of these foods than you have ever done before. The right kind of protein foods.

## Beware Hidden Fats

Many of our protein foods come laced with layers of heavy fat. Take so-called lean roast beef for instance. A hundred grammes of it will give you 28 grammes of good amino acids but will also deliver 31 grammes of fat which you decidedly don't need. A chicken leg of the same weight eaten skin and all brings 24 grammes of amino acids along with 21 grammes of fat.

There are other things to watch out for when eating meat and poultry (quite apart from whether or not you want or don't want to eat meat on moral grounds). Unless you are able to buy organic meat, the animals you will be eating have been raised on feeds laced with various chemicals. They are also frequently treated with antibiotics – all of which you ingest when you eat their flesh. All of these things you *don't* need if you are going to live a cellulite-free life. This doesn't mean that if you are a meat eater you must shun a delicious steak for the rest of your life but it does mean that you should be wise, indulge only occasionally and go for the best quality meat, preferably game.

Generally speaking better sources of amino acids come in the form of fish. There are 30 grammes of aminos with only 9 grammes of fat in a 100 gramme portion of plaice for instance, or 14 grammes in the same quantity of shrimp with only 3 grammes of fat, or 28 grammes of amino acids with only 9 grammes of fat in water-packed tuna.

If you prefer to get your aminos from vegetable sources you also need to be aware of the fat content. And you need skilfully to combine (not at the same meal, but within the same day) your grains and pulses to get a full complement of the amino acids your body needs to rebuild its tissues. For the amino acids found in vegetables and grains are in general not in the right proportions for the body to make full use of. The best vegetarian sources of aminos are those vegetables which contain more than 15 per cent protein: lentils, navy beans, split peas, kidney beans, soya beans, dried whole peas, lima beans. and wheat germ. When you take one of these foods at one meal and then at another meal take a good source of complex carbohydrate which is under 5 per cent fat, such as brown rice, whole wheat, steel-cut oats, whole buckwheat, whole corn or wild rice, the aminos that these different groups of foods contain complement the pulses and are able to supply your body with a good balance of amino acids for producing proteins, enzymes and all the rest. The only disadvantage with going the vegetarian route is that some people find pulses hard to digest (aloe vera can certainly help here) and some women find carbohydrates, even in their complex form such as whole grain breads and brown rice, tend to make them feel tired.

If you feel you must be vegetarian on moral grounds by all means go ahead. The world is full of beautiful women without cellulite who thrive on vegetarian fare. If not, however, at least during **The Breakdown** and **Buildup** periods in which you are actively shedding cellulite (and this can take several months for nature works slowly but surely), you might be better off exploring fish, shellfish and eggs as a source of protein as well as a little vegetarian miracle of nature called spirulina which has numerous other valuable attributes for combating cellulite.

## Nature's Green Miracle

A near-microscopic form of blue-green fresh-water algae, spirulina is made up of translucent bubble-thin cells stacked end to end to form an incredibly beautiful deep green helix. Spirulina is one specific form of blue-green algae of which there are more than 25,000 varieties on the earth. Some 3½ billion years ago these blue-green algae began to fix nitrogen from the atmosphere and to convert it into carbon dioxide and sugars and in the process release free oxygen. In time this created the oxygen-rich atmosphere in which the rest of life was able to develop. The whole process took over one billion years to complete.

So prolifically does spirulina grow when properly cultivated that an area only the size of Wales growing it could entirely feed 6 billion people – the estimated population of the planet by the year 2000. That is why spirulina is currently being investigated as at least part of the answer to protein and nutrient shortages in Third World countries. In Chad in Africa where it grows wild, it has been used for centuries as the major source of protein – eaten raw in the form of sun-dried patties which form naturally at the banks of the lakes in which it grows.

Spirulina is unique and remarkable in so many ways that it is hard to list them all but it is probably the single most important nutritional supplement you can use to support good body ecology in this age of pollution in which we live. When it comes to recreating cellulite-free flesh, it is something I would never do without. First, spirulina has a superior amino acid profile. Not only is it higher in complete bio-available protein than any other known food, it offers amino acids in a superb balance and in a form of protein which is easier to digest than any other kind. It is also lower in fat than any other kind. Finally, the protein in spirulina, unlike that in meat or fish or eggs or most vegetable foods, is *alkaline* in character rather than acid. This can be very important when you are in the process of detoxifying the body since most of the stored wastes you want to get rid of are acid in nature.

The amino acid balance in spirulina is unique – closest in its balance of one amino with another to that found in human breast milk. Many scientists are beginning to consider such a balance to be even better for human health than the balance of aminos you find in an egg, which for two generations now has been considered the ideal. Sixty to seventy per cent of spirulina consists of amino acids of the highest biological value (all eight aminos considered essential in correct proportions plus another 10), usable for building new body enzymes, tissues, cells and hormones. To give you some idea of just how extraordinary this is let's compare it to beef (18–22 per cent), soybeans (30–35 per cent), and eggs (12–16 per cent). Since all of the connective tissue, muscles and skin in your body is built primarily out of amino acids, such a potent source of well-balanced aminos in easily assimilated form can be very useful.

## Nutrients Par Excellence

This is only the beginning of the anti-cellulite spirulina story. Also contained within this extraordinary plant – a plant without leaves or roots, seeds, flowers or fruit that grows by the hundreds in a single drop of pure water – are some other wonderful nutrients in highly bio-available form which are particularly important for women's bodies. Take Vitamin B12 for instance – important in protecting you from anaemia.

Spirulina is nature's richest whole-food source of this vitamin. It is 2 to 6 times richer than raw beef liver which is generally touted as ideal. The iron content of spirulina is also the richest known in nature. Spirulina has 58 times more iron than raw spinach and 28 times more iron than raw beef liver. It is also the richest whole-food source of vitamin E (3 times richer than raw wheat germ), and of beta-carotene which is the precious anti-oxidant precursor of vitamin A so essential for building good skin and connective tissue (25 times richer than raw carrots). In truth, spirulina is nature's richest whole-food source of all the anti-oxidants since it contains just about every anti-oxidant known including the vitamins C, B1, B5 and B6, the minerals zinc, manganese and copper, the sulphur-based amino acid methionine and the trace element selenium, in addition to beta-carotene and vitamin E.

In the process of rebalancing body ecology and banishing cellulite you need quite literally to dissolve the old and build anew. Every minute 300,000,000 cells in your body wear out and die to be replaced. I know of no single food that can be of more help than spirulina in this process. Like sea plants, it also contains many rare and unique substances not found in other foods as well as all of the known nutrients – like chlorophyll, for example, and calcium. It is rich in phycocyanin, a blue pigment structurally similar to beta-carotene, which experiments have shown to enhance immune functions. (The immune system consists of your body's elaborate protective mechanisms which prevent infection, the onset of degenerative illnesses and premature ageing.)

Another special ingredient in spirulina is gamma linolenic acid or GLA which is found only in a few seeds and fruits (evening primrose oil is the best known source), and in human milk. GLA is essential to protect the integrity of the cells of the skin and muscles since it is an important ingredient in the formation of new cell walls. When cell walls are not well formed this can interfere with cell metabolism and the elimination of wastes, and lead to the buildup of polluted fluid around the cells and cellulite. What will probably surprise you is the fact that spirulina is also nature's richest whole-food source of GLA. The polyunsaturated oils in spirulina contain between 21 per cent and 29 per cent GLA – three times richer than the famous evening primrose oil (7–9 per cent).

## Eat Often And Well

In creating a new cellulite-free body ecology, it is essential that you rebuild new skin, connective tissue and muscles from protein foods which are high in bio-available amino acids. Frequent meals, however small, which are rich in these aminos not only spur the process but also help to balance blood-sugar fluctuations that otherwise can have you experiencing energy drains (most frequently late morning and mid-afternoons) and reaching for sweets or coffee just to keep going. No source of protein appears to be more bio-available than spirulina. Even the cell walls of this tiny plant are unique in that, instead of being made primarily from cellulose as are most plant cell walls, which demand that they be broken down during digestion, spirulina's cell walls are made up of mucopolysaccharides which dissolve immediately in the stomach to deliver all the nutritional goodness they contain to your system.

A teaspoon to a tablespoon of powdered spirulina in a glass of juice or a cup of vegetable broth is also just about the most energy-supporting thing you can do while on an anti-cellulite programme. It reduces your appetite naturally in case you are also trying to shed excess fat, it continues to supply a full complement of nutrients needed for body ecology balancing processes and (probably the most remarkable thing of all about the stuff) most women find that spirulina is the most satisfying food they have ever eaten. It is almost as though your body has been waiting for years for something that will support it so superbly and when it gets it, it simply laps it up with glee. This can eliminate much of the food craving and negative between-meal nibbling.

## Green Magic

How do you take spirulina? It is best taken in powder form either in juice or as a hot drink in vegetable broth – 3 or 4 times a day just as you might drink tea or coffee. You can also take it in tablet form but where in powder form it is absorbed almost on contact with the stomach, the tablets take around 45 minutes to get their goodness into your bloodstream. I have always found them nowhere near as satisfying. What I like to do is make up a big thermos of broth for the whole day to which I have added spirulina and then drink it whenever I need an energy boost or am slightly hungry. It is best to mix it with the broth powder and water just off the boil in a food processor then pour the mixture into the thermos. If you take it in juice, you can pour it into a jar or plastic cocktail shaker and then shake for a moment until the fine green powder is fully mixed.

How much? Start with 1 heaped teaspoon of spirulina to a glass of juice and work up to a heaped tablespoon. If you prefer to use the tablets (which are good to carry about in a handbag and take with water or herb tea), you will need 8 to 9 tablets to equal 1 rounded teaspoon (13 to 15 equals 1 rounded table-spoon). I would suggest starting with 1 teaspoon three or four times a day and working up to 1 tablespoon each time. Don't be put off by the slightly sea-like smell the first time you make a cup of the deep green spirulina broth (1 rounded teaspoon of broth powder to 1 rounded teaspoon–1 rounded tablespoon of spir-ulina). The drink tastes completely different. Spirulina is unquestionably one of the planet's finest natural complexes for supporting body ecology and the energy-enhancing health it creates at the highest levels.

## Let The Buyer Beware

As with all the wonderful complexes from nature, it is essential that you choose very carefully what kind of spirulina you buy (see Resources, page 84). A few years ago when somebody discovered that spirulina was a great natural appetite suppressant a lot of unscrupulous people got in on the act and started growing the stuff in ponds and lakes where the water was not absolutely pure. This means unfortunately that much spirulina still on the market is not abso-lutely pure but may contain traces of chemicals to pol-lute your body – even many of the good health-food supplement producers who label the product do not realize that what they are selling is not always of the best quality. So buy only the best. You deserve noth-ing less.

## Chapter Six
### THE ENERGIZE

# Energy to Burn

Despite all those books and articles that would have you believe otherwise, your body, like every living organism, is nothing like a machine. Use a machine – even skilfully – and it wears out. Use your body skilfully and it only gets stronger. To that you can add 'leaner', 'firmer', 'sleeker' and all the other attributes associated with cellulite-free flesh.

The emphasis is on the word 'skilfully'. Just what *is* skilful use? First let's look at what it is not. It is *not* body building based on *isometric* exercise. Isometrics heighten muscle tension without shortening muscle length thereby increasing peripheral vascular resistance without a significant increase in cardiac output. This kind of exercise which includes much body building and weight lifting (or even gritting your teeth and pushing against the wall) will make your muscles bigger and stronger but it will not improve what is called your cardiorespiratory conditioning: it will not make your heart and lungs stronger. Neither will it help detoxify your body and keep it clean from the inside out. Quite the opposite, isometrics tends to encourage the buildup of stasis in the tissues in certain areas of your body, locking in stored wastes and water instead of liberating them.

## Fit All Over

Exercise used as part of a programme to banish cellulite and keep it away needs above all to do the opposite. That is why it needs to be *isotonic* in nature. This means it needs to take you through large movements such as running, walking briskly, rebounding on a mini-trampoline, rowing, swimming and cycling which shorten and lengthen your muscles rhythmically without bringing about a big increase in tension. In very simple terms, you need to exercise so that you become fit all over, not just to concentrate on one area of your body. Why? Several reasons. First, regular aerobic isotonic exercise is one of the finest ways for a living organism to eliminate wastes before they have a chance to build up. Second, well-conditioned women who have lower heart rates than those of us who tend to be sedentary also show decreased activity of the sympathetic nervous system which means they are better able to deal with stress of all kinds without experiencing the buildup of negative chemical by-products in their system to disrupt good body ecology. Finally, they have far better VO2-Max.

## De-ageing Your Body

VO2-Max is the best overall indication of your physical fitness. It is a measurement of just how much oxygen you are able to consume. A high consumption of oxygen is essential not only to maintaining a cellulite-free body but also to keeping muscle and bone tissue healthy, to ensuring that skin remains relatively unwrinkled, firm and thick and to avoiding the progressive stiffness in your joints that is associated with age.

VO2-Max declines with age so that, for instance, a woman of 60 has only two-thirds the VO2-Max of a 20 year old. This decline is much slower in women who exercise regularly. But it can happen fast too. For instance, if you are bedridden for three weeks your VO2-Max can fall by 20–25 per cent. That is the bad news. The good news is even better: a sedentary woman who begins a programme of *moderate* exercise can increase her VO2-Max by as much as 30–40 per cent, bringing vast quantities of oxygen to serve her metabolic processes, rebalancing her body's ecology and quite literally rejuvenating herself while helping to shift cellulite.

The key to it all is the word *moderate*. Ever since Dr Kenneth Cooper published his revolutionary book *Aerobics* in 1968, and men and women in the Western world became fascinated with exploring what exercise can do to transform body and mind, we have been obsessed with the notion (quite false) that the harder you work at aerobic exercise the better the results you will get. You know the kind of thing: grit your teeth, force yourself and unless it hurts you are not getting any real benefit from it. Nothing could be further from the truth. Especially when you are talking about cellulite-prone women or women with a tendency to gain and keep excess fat in their bodies. It is important that you understand once and for all why this is so although you may have to deal with some unfamiliar terms and wrestle with some of the metabolic processes that are at the centre of maintaining good body ecology along the way. So please bear with me.

The skeletal muscles of your body are made up of two kinds of fibre: red (type I) and white (type II). The red fibres are high in myoglobin, in mitochondria (the cells' fat-burning factories) and in oxidative capacity. This means that they tend to burn fat to fuel their movement. They are also low in glycolytic sugar-burning enzymes and they are slow to contract. White fibres on the other hand are lower in myoglobin,

50

mitochondria and oxidative capacity but high in glycolytic enzymes. When you work your body hard – going for broke and pushing to your limits – you are treating it as a sprinter does. Sprinters have a lot of white muscle fibres in comparison to red while long-distance runners have a preponderance of red.

## Burning Fat Not Sugar

Your skeletal muscles contain only limited quantities of the high-energy phosphate compounds such as creatine phosphate (CP) and adenosine triphosphate (ATP) that you need to generate more energy to feed the movement when exerting your body. There are three ways of doing this: you can call on glycogen or sugar stored in the muscles, or you can call on glucose – sugar stored in the blood – or you can call on free fatty acids (FFA) which you get either from triglycerides stored in the body or from burning fatty tissues via the mitochondria.

Which route you use to feed your movements depends on the intensity of the effort you are making in your exercise. Using exercise to enhance body ecology, and thereby both to decrease cellulite and to rejuvenate, demands *low intensity* not the push-to-the-limits self-punishing thrust that so many exercise enthusiasts propound with a passion bordering on the fanatical. Why? Because low-intensity isotonic movement develops red not white muscle fibre and burns fat best. To be more specific it utilizes free fatty acids first and only second does it turn to muscle glycogen as food. That is exactly what you are after in breaking down cellulite as well as in shedding ordinary fat from the body. Whether or not you are overweight, you want to stimulate the mitochondria of your cells to release fatty acids, turning them into energy and

51

enhancing metabolic processes at a cellular level, so that all of the areas of your body in which there is a reduced-energy stasis (rather like stagnant ponds on the earth) become active. If you happen to be over-weight as well, you will also get maximum support for the burning of stored fat and for turning flabby low-energy tissue into firm strong muscle as a bonus.

If you go the other route with exercise, if you push yourself to your limits in the belief that you will burn more calories or follow the philosophy of 'the more the better', you will only defeat your every effort to shed peau d'orange thighs. As aerobic exercise increases, more white fibres develop and the burning of glycogen becomes more important that the burning of fat.

Science measures all this quite precisely. At 80 per cent of your exercise limit glycogen supplies twice the energy that fat-free fatty acids do. At 100 per cent capacity it supplies virtually all. Pushing yourself to your limits only make worse the disturbances in your body's ecology which produced cellulite in the first place. It also produces large quantities of lactic acid creating acidosis, which further limits your muscular performance and increases your bodily pollution. (That is why, alas, a few top women athletes can't shift their cellulite.)

## Set Your Own Targets

Exercise to banish cellulite needs to be rhythmical and continuous, to use large muscle groups and to be performed at an intensity and frequency that increases your heart output only to *60 per cent of maximum heart rate* (MHR) – never more.

How do you find out just what this means for you? Simple. First learn to take your own pulse. Place 3 fingers along the artery at the wrist until you feel the steady beat of your heart. Then, using a watch with a second hand, count how many times your heart beats while the second hand records six seconds passing. Finally, multiply by 10. This will tell you how many beats per minute your heart is beating. Once you know how to do this it is easy to calculate the rest.

To discover your maximum heart rate, subtract your age from 220. Then multiply this figure by 0.6. This will give you your *target heart rate* (THR). For instance, if you are 40 years old:

MHR = 220 – 40 = 180 beats per minute (BPM)

180 BPM x 60% = 108 BPM

Therefore any form of sustained aerobic exercise which gets your heart beating at around 108 beats per minute is ideal for minimizing the buildup of wastes in your system that contribute to cellulite buildup, for releasing wastes already stored in your tissues, and for burning any excess fat present. Whenever you are exercising, stop for a moment and measure your pulse to see that it hovers around this level, give or take 10 beats per minute. Then you will know you are on the right track.

## The Joy Factor

What kind of exercise is best? The kind you *like* best. For the joy factor is a vital ingredient in de-polluting a body and rebalancing ecology. Try walking briskly in comfortable clothing and low-heeled shoes, cross-country skiing on one of those new-fangled machines which simulate the real thing, dancing, cycling, rowing, swimming, skating, hiking or rebounding on a mini-trampoline. (More about this very special kind of exercise on page 59 – in many ways the best in the world for women wanting to banish cellulite even if they exercise regularly in other ways too.

How long should you work out? From 15 to 60 minutes at a session. More is *not* necessarily better. You need to judge how long is right for you by checking on how fatigued you feel one hour after completing an exercise session. That is the best indication of whether or not you are working *with* your body's own rhythms and needs. But begin slowly with only 15 to 20 minutes. Remember to check on your heart rate at least twice during every exercise session and adjust your activity accordingly when it goes more than ten beats above or below your target rate. As you get fitter and fitter you may want to exercise for more time. But if you find yourself fatigued an hour after an exercise session then you are overdoing it. So pull back until your body is ready for a higher dose of activity.

Just as working too hard – pushing your heart rate above your target heart rate – is counterproductive to banishing cellulite, so is working too long. Exercise done properly will energize, not exhaust you. If an hour after a session you feel a lot of fatigue that is a sure sign you have been pushing too hard. Your body has probably been burning sugar rather than fat and in the process producing 'clinkers' of waste which will undermine your body's ability to shed cellulite.

How often? Three to five times a week. Always leave no more than 48 hours between sessions so that you will continue to benefit from the enhanced metabolic rate that low-intensity aerobic isotonic exercise creates in your body. Start slowly. When you notice positive changes in energy taking place in your body and an enhanced self-awareness as you get into an exercise programme, you will find your body craving more. Then go for it – but slowly and gently, always keeping within your own target heart rate.

## New Sources of Power

There is something wonderful about exercising in this way if you are a woman. Even women who have all but lost a sense of intuitive connection with their bodies often find they rediscover it. Frequently, women begin for the first time lovingly, gently and effectively to care for themselves instead of either neglecting their deepest needs or slave-driving themselves to keep up with some imagined image of womanhood created by the media. For advertising and media fantasies, although frequently subliminally, are always implying that each woman in her own unique shape and style is somehow not good enough – and therefore that she needs the latest expensive cream, eyeshadow or designer suit to be acceptable. This kind of thing *dis-empowers* a woman, teaching her not to trust her body or her instincts. Following this kind of exercise programme leads you to experience an increasing sense of your own power and to sense a profound connection to the life processes on which good looks, mental clarity, high-level health and resistance to cellulite and to early ageing depend. Care for yourself in this way and you will begin to experience an abundance of life force and creativity that you can use in any way you wish. Go for it.

## Chapter Seven

# THE SMOOTHOUT

# **Body Sculpture**

Not all the power to render flesh cellulite-free comes from inside. The kind of work you do on the surface of your body through massage, movement and hydrotherapy plays a central role in establishing good body ecology and eliminating puckered thighs. Good outer treatments stimulate the metabolism, creating more energy both at a cellular level and in the body as a whole; help break down damaged and disordered connective tissue thus detoxifying stagnant areas of flesh and clearing the way for **The Rebuild**; and, in many ways most important of all, stimulate lymphatic drainage – central to keeping your body internally clean.

## **Lymphomania**

Your body is more than 70 per cent water. So important is water to the processes of life that according to Nobel laureate Albert Szent-Györgyi, 'Life is water dancing to the tune of solids.' A French biologist named Oliviero rather poetically reinforced Szent-Györgyi's observation by saying, 'Man is an amphibian. Even the most beautiful woman's body is no more

56

than 50 litres of lukewarm sea water in which trillions of cells live and fight for survival.'

Five litres of this 'sea water' are found in your blood and five in digestive and other secretions. Almost all the rest make up your lymphatic fluid or lymph – sometimes called 'white blood'. Thanks to this lymph, a ceaseless interchange goes on between your body's trillions of cells and their surrounding interstitial fluids. Food and oxygen are exchanged for waste products eliminated from the cells – all via the medium of water.

## The Exchange Rate

Nutrients and oxygen are transported to the tissues and cells via the bloodstream. Arterial pressure forces the blood through 10 billion tiny capillaries and out into the cells' interstitial spaces there to effect an exchange with wastes which the cells have produced. Then the water or interstitial fluid filled with these wastes and toxic products is gathered by tiny lymphatic tubules and sent back through the lymph vessels to be detoxified.

The lymphatics consist of a highly organized and elaborate system of ducts and channels which flow throughout your body. In fact almost all the tissues of the body are equipped with lymph channels which drain excess fluid and the wastes which it contains from the interstitial spaces. This opalescent liquid from these minute channels transports wastes and toxic products into larger lymphatic vessels on through lymph nodes located in the groin, under the arm and in the neck. There it undergoes a process of purification and, once clean, is channelled back into the blood.

To maintain good body ecology – for cells and tissues to be nourished so that they remain vital, and your flesh and skin and muscles smooth and cellulite-free – this interchange needs to occur without impediments such as a metabolic slowdown, or hardened connective tissue which traps water and wastes around the cells, or lack of tone in the muscles. The 'water' itself also needs to be relatively uncontaminated and you need good lymphatic drainage to keep these fluids carrying wastes away. It is your body's lymph system which provides all this – a system very different in nature from blood circulation where arterial pressure from the heart beating forces blood through tiny capillaries in your body.

Your lymphatic system has no prime mover. Instead, its nourishing, water-balancing and elimination functions are almost entirely dependent upon gravity and on the natural pressure of muscles that takes place when you move your body. That is one of the reasons why regular aerobic exercise, such as taking long walks in comfortable shoes, is so important in encouraging the steady and effective elimination of wastes from your cells and tissues. Lymph circulates very slowly. This becomes even slower when you are tired or cold, or sedentary or under stress, all of which contribute to an accumulation of waste products in the tissues and a buildup of stasis where stagnant water creates oedema. Wherever cellulite is present, lymphatic drainage needs improvement.

## Make A Friend Of Gravity

Inverting your body temporarily can help a lot to encourage good lymph flow. You can even raise the bottom of your bed a foot off the floor or lie in a hammock with your feet high for a few minutes a couple of times a day. Lying with your feet higher than your head reverses the flow of lymph temporarily and helps improve lymphatic drainage. It is particularly helpful to do for 20 minutes a day if you tend to get water retention in your legs which makes them feel heavy and tired and makes ankles swell mildly – particularly in the evening. But gravity can be a help in another way when it comes to enhancing lymph cleansing and eliminating cellulite.

Rebounding – bouncing up and down on a mini trampoline – is the best form of exercise you can get to help **The Smoothout**. It is also more fun, I think, than any other kind. When you are at the top of a bounce your body is completely weightless like an astronaut in space. When you come down against the trampoline, gravity exerts a force of 2 to 3 Gs so that bouncing brings a constant rhythm of pressure and release. On the upward movement gravity closes up the millions of one-way valves which control the flow of lymph. Then when you come down again onto the mat internal pressure changes quickly and dramatically, causing them to open and bringing about a surge of lymph so that you set up an internal 'massaging motion' which shunts lymph along. Rebounding is an excellent way to begin the day, say, for 10 minutes before breakfast. It really gets your body and mind working and seems to raise spirits like nothing else I have ever come across. It can also be useful to do for 10 minutes or more at other times of the day particularly when you are feeling down or fatigued. I like to keep my rebounder in front of the television set and to watch good films on video while using it.

## The Medium Is Massage

Lymphatic drainage massage is a series of slow pumping movements following the rhythm of lymph in order to encourage its flow. It can help a lot if you know someone who can give it to you since it is very difficult to do on oneself. So can gentle circular movements on the thighs and tummy, buttocks and lower legs using one of the anti-cellulite devices (See Resources, page 84). They vary tremendously in design and effectiveness – from electrical mits that dispense their own anti-cellulite oil and German whirling rods covered with hundreds of tiny silver spikes to ridged devices which you rub over your flesh either on their own or in conjunction with an external anti-cellulite product. An ideal way to use these devices is after a shower or bath which you have preceded by a couple of minutes of skin brushing with a dry natural bristle brush (see page 20).

And what about the proprietary anti-cellulite products? Some are useless and some are very good. They are not some cosmetic con either. One of the biggest hypocrisies going in the cosmetic industry is the notion that the skin will not absorb active ingredients. It is a hypocrisy on which the very definition of cosmetic depends. For if cosmetic companies were to admit that many of the best skincare and bodycare products they make are absorbed far deeper than the epidermis then they would be accused of making drugs and have to pull their products off the market. The next time somebody tries to tell you nothing you put on the surface of your body will do anything either for cellulite or skincare you have a perfect right to tell them they don't know what they are talking about. So effectively can the skin absorb some substances that physicians rubbed oil-based vitamins on to the thighs of malnourished concentration camp victims who were unable to digest food in order to cure vitamin deficiencies.

## Lotions and Potions

The active ingredients in the best of the cellulite creams, lotions and oils include a number of potent herbal extracts to help enhance circulation, encourage lipolysis (fat burning), restore integrity to damaged capillaries, decrease waterlogging and improve firmness. They include things like silica derivatives, free form amino acids, herbal extracts from butcher's broom to horsetail and even caffeine (which applied in the right form to the surface of the skin has been shown quite clearly to stimulate fat burning). The trouble with all of the creams and potions is that, like the special treatments for cellulite you can get from a doctor or a beauty therapist, including liposuction multi-injector syringe treatments, lymphatic drainage massage, ionithermie and the rest, they will only work together with a total body programme. The other trouble is that these treatments, like anti-cellulite products, are often expensive.

You can make one of your own, however, which works even better than most of the fancy ones at a fraction of the cost. It is true it will not have a sweet cosmetic smell like the others and because it contains herbal extracts which are brown in colour, you will need to be careful not to stain the white bathroom rug when applying it. But it works a treat. Here's how to make it.

Take 1 small bottle of aloe vera liquid (350ml). Add to it 25ml of liquid extract of *fucus vesculosus* and 25ml of kola liquid extract. Shake well. Keep refrigerated. Apply twice a day to cellulite-prone areas of the body after a bath or shower; then, using one of the special anti-cellulite gloves or mits or rollers, gently go over important areas of your body.

## Water Works

Water is a powerful energy-balancer – so good that most people who begin to experiment with hydrotherapy techniques are astounded by what they can do. Hot and cold water applied alternately to the surface of your skin stimulates circulation through the cardiovascular system and spurs good lymphatic drainage. From an electromagnetic point of view, by energizing these systems you are increasing electricity at the heart of your cells – the mitochondria – and thereby heightening your body's ability to produce energy at a cellular level. This in turn increases over-all physical vitality. But hydrotherapy works in another way too. Like a diet high in fresh green vegetables and low in processed convenience foods and sugar, it also helps detoxify acid wastes which are interfering with normal energetic processes.

## Blitzguss

Hydrotherapy in one form or another is a must both for helping to prevent cellulite and for restoring cellulite-riddled tissues to normal. It enhances circulation, eliminates stored wastes, increases energy exchange on a cellular level and even heightens immunity. The best water treatment for cellulite is the traditional German Blitzguss. A *real* one needs to be done by a professional but you can get many of the same effects in the shower yourself at home – especially if you have a hand-held shower which you can direct on different parts of your body. Here's how.

Take a warm shower until your skin is really glowing with warmth. Then turn off the hot water and using only cold, direct it over your face and then down your arms and legs, over your trunk and abdomen and down your back. Finally, concentrate on the areas of your body where cellulite accumulates – the thighs, abdomen, hips and buttocks. The whole process should take no more than 30 seconds. Then get out of the shower, pat off the excess water and dress warmly. Do this at least once a day after skin brushing.

## Beautiful Baths

Epsom salts baths which are used in **The Breakdown** are excellent tools for **The Smoothout** as well. Use them when you are tense or fatigued. Seaweed baths and peat baths can also be helpful for the stimulation they give locally to cells beneath the surface of the skin and for their ability to encourage the elimination of wastes through the skin's surface. Use them frequently (ideally three times a week) but always make sure they are taken at just above blood heat and that you remain in the water for at least 20 minutes – the time it takes for your body to react to whatever you have submerged it in. The most important thing of all about using external tools and treatments is that you use them over and over again regularly with no breaks in between. It is this kind of consistency which really brings results. It took a long while for cellulite to develop and nature's processes work slowly but surely so stay with it.

Chapter Eight

THE REBALANCE

# The Eating Revolution

A major focus of anti-cellulite advice in recent years has revolved around diet – and quite right too. By now it goes without saying that if you value good looks, longevity and energy, and if you seek protection from premature ageing, there are certain basic principles you want to follow. These include cutting out nutritionally depleted, highly processed and refined foods – from corn flakes to biscuits, sweets, white bread and white pasta. Similarly you want to avoid tinned, smoked and chemically treated foods, most red meat (unless it is organic and very lean such as game) white sugar, excess tea or coffee, and taking lots of alcohol. All of this falls under the category of 'good advice for health and good looks' so, yes, by all means follow it. But using diet specifically to get rid of cellulite, and keep it away, is quite a lot more skilful than that – more about that in a moment.

## Sodium-Potassium Suppositions

Many cellulite 'experts' go to great lengths to tell you that you must cut down on (some even say cut *out*) salt. Why? Sodium and potassium are antagonistic elements in the body which means that they need to balance each other for you to be healthy. The daily intake of potassium in Britain is estimated to be between 2 and 4 grammes a day, the daily intake of sodium between 3 and 6 grammes. A good balance between sodium and potassium in your body is essential for good health and there is growing evidence that people on a Western diet of convenience and highly processed foods heavily laden with salt are not getting as much potassium as they need. Most of the potassium in your body is found inside your cells in a sodium:potassium ratio of 1:10. Most of the sodium is found outside your cells at a ratio of 28:1.

The difference in concentration between inside and outside across the cell membrane is actively maintained by what is known as the *sodium pump* which is the biochemical mechanism that regulates the taking into the cells of the nutrients needed for health and removing waste products. If the sodium-potassium balance in your body gets out of kilter you get a swelling of the cells, as occurs frequently in cellulite, the retention of water and wastes in the interstitial spaces and a decrease in the electrical potential across the cell membrane – all of which contribute to cellulite.

## Go For The Good Guys

You don't need to rush out and buy all the strange 'low-sodium' products recommended on some anti-cellulite diets including those ghastly tasting salt substitutes – far from it. Provided you select your foods from the 'good guys' to begin with, i.e. lots of fresh vegetables, only whole grains, fish, free-range eggs and poultry, and you steer clear of the refined sugars, pre-cooked packaged foods and junk foods, you will get plenty of potassium, not too much sodium and will never have to worry about it at all. For what many of the anti-sodium fanatics forget is that it is not only an upset in the sodium-potassium balance which can cause the swelling of fat cells and the buildup of water in the interstitial areas. So can kidneys in poor condition, taking aspirin frequently, certain gastrointestinal disorders and the use of diuretics. Another culprit can be a deficiency in some of the co-factors needed to fuel enzymes such as B6 or zinc, or of certain essential fatty acids, or a difficulty changing the essential fatty acid linolenic acid into gamma linolenic acid in your body (the stuff you find in evening primrose oil). Since the cell walls of skin and muscle tissue involved in cellulite are made up mostly of fatty acids, when your body does not have an adequate supply or when you have been eating a lot of fried foods which interfere with its ability to absorb essential fatty acids from your foods, then the integrity of the cell walls is breached resulting in the leakage of fluids and in inefficient production of energy within the cells. So forget all the panic about salt and all the worry about fancy low-sodium foods and simply eat well, getting lots of fresh vegetables – the more the better. Unless you have a real medical problem, which should be treated by your doctor anyway, you shouldn't need to worry about the rest.

## Energy Efficiency At Its Best

Lots of what we eat these days is 'on the run'. It is eaten quickly, is poorly chewed and often taken in a stressful environment whether you are a mother at home trying to feed demanding children, a working woman doing your best to cope with a packed lunch while the phone rings or someone in an overcrowded restaurant having to shout to be heard across the table. Chewing well is the first step to good digestion. It decreases the size of food particles, increasing their surface area for enzymes to do the breaking down they need to so you can take in all the nutrients the foods offer you without building up excessive wastes. It also initiates the digestion of carbohydrates by the salivary amylase enzymes that are released in the chewing process. When you consume a lot of fat (and in Britain more than 40 per cent of our calories come from fats), this can cut down by half the meal-stimulated secretion of gastric acid and the enzyme pepsin in the stomach so you do not break down your foods profitably and do not get all the nutrients you need to support good body ecology. This situation also produces an excess of waste in the form of poorly digested and assimilated foods for your cells and body as a whole to deal with – wastes that only contribute further to cellulite.

What is less known is that when lots of fat or carbohydrate – particularly refined carbohydrates such as white bread and pasta, sugary products and over-processed foods – are taken with a concentrated protein, a significant retardation of protein digestion often results in a similar buildup of wastes as a consequence. This recent understanding of some of the factors which influence or interfere with good breakdown and absorption of nutrients from foods sheds some light on why the old naturopathic concept of food combining works to encourage maximal digestion and detoxification, and minimizes the buildup of wastes in the whole body. It may be why the practice of conscientious food combining (where you do not mix concentrated starches such as potatoes, beans, pulses, chickpeas, rice, wheat oats and so forth with concentrated proteins such as fish, game, shellfish, poultry etc.) has over generations shown itself to be an effective general approach to many chronic problems from poor digestion and fatigue to rheumatic conditions. When it comes to eating to help banish cellulite and keep it at bay, there is nothing better.

## Almost Easy As Pie

Pie, by the way, is one thing you can't eat when conscientiously combining your foods, nor quiche, nor pasta with cheese. They are all excellent examples of poorly combined foods which mix concentrated proteins with concentrated carbohydrates or starches – each of which tends to interfere with the full breakdown of the other except in those rare people lucky enough to have the digestive capacity of a rhinoceros who can manage just about anything without difficulty. So, have your whole-grain bread or potatoes, or rice with a salad and cooked vegetables at one meal and at another take your fish or eggs or game again with fresh vegetables. Just don't mix them together. Then you will get maximum nutrition out of everything you eat and you will minimize the buildup of waste both in your cells and in your body as a whole. Eating in this way over a few weeks also increases your body's ability to eliminate easily any wastes which are present so they don't contribute to the buildup of cellulite in the tissues.

## Slimmer's Bonus

Conscientious food combining has some wonderful bonuses too – increased energy levels for instance.

And, if you are someone who, as part of your programme for eliminating cellulite, needs to shed excess fat as well, you will be delighted to learn that many women find simply eliminating junk foods, over-processed foods and refined foods, and separating their concentrated proteins from their concentrated starches as well as increasing the quantity of fresh raw vegetables they eat, results in permanent weight loss without ever having to count calories again. I discovered this several years ago for myself and then wrote a book on slimming using these principles called **The Biogenic Diet**. Since it has appeared I have had scores of letters from women each confirming in their own words the way in which even highly resistant fat can be shed automatically without ever having to consciously restrict amounts.

When using conscientious food combining specifically for cellulite there is one further addition you might like to make – that of sea plants in the form of seaweeds, algae, kelp and all the rest. Add them to your soups, soak them in water and then tuck them into your salads and take them as nutritional supplements. Two peoples in the world understand the powers of sea plants better than any others: the French and the Japanese. the French have for generations used seaweeds as nutritional supplements in atomized form both internally and in active anti-cellulite baths. The Japanese rely on masses of sea plants of all varieties to give them a superb balance of essential minerals and trace elements. Sea plants belong on any anti-cellulite programme. They are rich in organic iodine, the element central to the functioning of the thyroid on which overall body metabolism depends. They are also rich in forms of soluble fibre called the alginates which have an ability to bind and remove heavy metals from the body These heavy metals can block important metabolic pathways and contribute to free radical damage which produces premature ageing. So they offer powerful help for detoxification at the deepest levels.

## Precious Iodine

When there is any deficiency of iodine (and there is every indication that our diet contains less and less as our soils become depleted), then the thyroid cannot function properly and your body's ability to burn calories for energy is impeded. French internal and external treatments for cellulite rely heavily on the stimulating effects of organic iodine in the sea plants which they use in baths for their ability to stimulate cellular metabolism via the skin. (In order for this to work, by the way, the algae in question need to be specially treated to microlize them – break them into microscopic particles so that the content of these plant cells can be absorbed through the exterior of the body.) There are a number of different kinds of sea plants you can incorporate into your diet to great effect (your nails and hair and skin will benefit too). Explore the different varieties – from nori which you can toast quickly and then flick over salads, to orami which is excellent in soups. Alternatively, or in conjunction with these, you can take a good supplement of sea plants, but it has to be made from algae taken from *unpolluted* waters. It should be in concentrated form and it should be atomized into microscopic particles for easy absorption of its precious minerals. A mixture of several different kinds of algae is best since each kind has something of particular value to offer (see Resources, page 85).

## New Flesh From New Life Habits

The whole point about conscientious food combining is that it is not a way of eating where you have to deprive yourself of something, grit your teeth and bear it. Once you have tossed all the junk food from your larder (and you haven't a hope in hell of getting rid of cellulite without eliminating it from your life), it all takes very little discipline. Eat as much as you like but simply rearrange *what* you eat *when*. It takes a couple of weeks to get the hang of it all – then it becomes very easy indeed for you can go anywhere and eat anything so long as it is simple wholesome food. Because of the support it offers in terms of enhancing digestive breakdown, for many women this way of eating also clears up that awful craving where one biscuit leads to a whole package and then feeling bad about yourself because you don't seem to have any 'willpower'. Conscientious food combining can change all that for many people within a couple of weeks. And to anyone who has long fought with it this can sometimes seem the greatest blessing of all.

# Conscientious Food Combining

To get into a way of eating for sleek smooth thighs and long-term wellbeing, follow these simple guidelines:

- Eliminate all highly processed foods and junk foods from your larder including boxed breakfast cereals like corn flakes, breads made from refined flour, white pasta, white sugar and all the so-called goodies made from it.

- Cut way back on tea and coffee. If you drink either, make it organic so you avoid taking in any more chemicals and pesticides than absolutely necessary. And drink no more than a cup or two a day.

- Restrict your alcohol to a glass (occasionally 2 at the most) of *good* wine with a meal once a day.

- Never eat a concentrated starch food with a concentrated protein food at the same meal. (Nix on fish and chips or roast beef and Yorkshire pudding.)

- Serve only one concentrated protein food or one concentrated starch food per meal, i.e. don't mix your carpaccio starter with a turbot main dish or eat your bread with potatoes.

- Leave at least 4 to 5 hours between a starch meal and a protein one.

- Eat fruit on its own or leave at least 20 to 30 minutes between a fruit starter and the next course of your meal.

- Eat only fruit for breakfast plus your spirulina in fruit juice or broth and your organic silica. Because of the easy digestibility of spirulina and its alkaline nature (quite unique in the protein world of food), it can be taken with impunity. The liver, which is your body's chemical factory behind the whole detoxification process, is most active between midnight and midday and you want to support its actions. Your body can digest a fruit meal without bringing into play a lot of digestive enzymes, allowing the liver to get on with the detoxification process instead of having to turn its attention to digestion. The fruit breakfast – as much as you like including a fruit snack mid-morning if you want – encourages detoxification while the spirulina and silica help rebuild what needs rebuilding and also keep you from feeling hungry.

- Make one meal a day a *huge* raw salad full of all kinds of fresh vegetables. It provides fibre for elimination of wastes and also lots of important minerals and vitamins.

- Chew well!

You can pick and choose your own foods and make up your own menus provided you follow the basic principles of conscientious food combining (see chart). But here are what a week's sample menus might look like – just for inspiration:

## FIRST DAY

**Breakfast:**

Fresh fruit, either as it comes or made into a fruit frappé or fruit salad. Eat as much as you like but chew well so you get all the goodness out of every bite. If you are hungry later have another couple of pieces mid-morning as well. If you choose melon as your fruit then don't mix it with other fruits – eat it on its own or leave it alone. Supplements can be mixed with broth and drunk as a hot drink if you like.

**Lunch:**

Fresh spinach salad with toasted rye bread spread with chopped black olive paste.

Herb tea. Supplements.

**Supper:**

Poached salmon with mayonnaise, steamed broccoli with mushrooms, a sprout salad with olive oil, lemon and Worcester sauce dressing.

Herb tea. Supplements.

You may include a glass of wine.

## SECOND DAY

**Breakfast:**

As for day one.

**Lunch:**

Avocado, tomato and mozzarella salad.

Herb tea. Supplements.

**Supper:**

Stir-fried vegetables including orami seaweed with brown rice and watercress salad.

Herb tea. Supplements.

You may include a glass of wine.

## THIRD DAY

**Breakfast:**
As for day one.
**Lunch:**
Corn Soup with a big watercress salad and fennel.
Herb tea. Supplements.
**Supper:**
Melon to start. (Be sure to leave 20 minutes between the melon and your main course.)
Grilled chicken with mange tout, carrots and baby onions.
Herb tea. Supplements.
You may include a glass of wine.

## FOURTH DAY

**Breakfast:**
As for day one.
**Lunch:**
Large bowl of crudités with soya cottage cheese, mayonnaise or garlic dip.
Herb tea. Supplements.
**Supper:**
Spicy fish kebabs with mixed green salad and giant mushrooms grilled in lemon and garlic.
Herb tea. Supplements.
You may include a glass of wine.

## FIFTH DAY

**Breakfast:**
As for day one.
**Lunch:**
Bulgar wheat salad with carrots, raw beetroot, parsley and chives.
Herb tea. Supplements.

**Supper:**
Jerusalem artichoke salad with light vinaigrette dressing.
King prawns grilled in olive oil and garlic, braised
fennel, endive and ruccola.
Herb tea. Supplements.
You may include a glass of wine.

## SIXTH DAY

**Breakfast:**
As for day one.
**Lunch:**
Baked potato with chopped tomatoes, onions and
avocado with fresh basil and olive oil.
Herb tea. Supplements.
**Supper:**
Grilled mackerel with steamed broccoli, carrots and
swede. Mixed salad.
Herb tea. Supplements.
You may include a glass of wine.

## SEVENTH DAY

**Breakfast:**
As for day one.
**Lunch:**
Autumn vegetable soup.
Radiccio and chopped egg salad with avocado dressing.
Herb tea. Supplements.
**Supper:**
Crudité.
Braised breast of duck. A selection of baked vegetables
– onion, parsnips and leeks.
Herb tea. Supplements.
You may include a glass of wine.

## PROTEINS

nuts ☆ seeds
dairy produce
eggs · game · fish
shellfish · poultry
etc...

## CONSCIENTIOUS FOOD - COMBINING CHART

← POOR →

## STARCHES

potatoes
beans & pulses
grains · pumpkin
sweet potatoes
etc...

GOOD

GOOD

SUB-ACID & SWEET FRUITS

FAIR

SUB-ACID & SWEET FRUITS

POOR

## ★ VEGETABLES ★

asparagus · aubergine
beetroot · carrot · peas
leafy greens · sweet corn
salad vegetables · turnip
etc...

GOOD

FAIR

FAIR

## ACID FRUITS

strawberries
lemon · lime
orange · plum
raspberries
pineapple

GOOD

## SUB-ACID FRUITS

apple
apricot
peach · grapes
mango · cherries

FAIR

## SWEET FRUITS ☆

banana · dates
raisins &
other dried
fruits etc...

FAIR

## ★ MELONS ★

eat on their
own or leave
alone.

## RECOMMENDATION

make meals of one or two
combinations, especially
of one protein or one
starch with one or
two vegetables

## COMBINATIONS

POOR

fruit & starch
protein & starch

FAIR

leafy greens & acid fruits
leafy greens & sub-acid
fruits · protein &
acid fruits.

GOOD

avocado & acid or sub-
acid fruits · avocado
& leafy vegetables
protein & leafy greens,
starch & vegetables.
oils & leafy greens,
oils & acid or sub-acid
fruits.

## NEUTRAL FOODS

(they go well with
anything)
avocado olives
seed oils.

all juices can
be mixed
because they are
liquid and can be
absorbed by the body
within half an hour.

## Chapter Ten

## THE RECLAIM

# The Power of Deep Ecology

How often do you rejoice in your body? How often do you feel absolutely at ease in your skin, at peace in yourself and in harmony with your world with or without peau d'orange thighs? This is something very important if you want your flesh to remain cellulite-free.

It is interesting that cellulite which is so common in Europe and the United States is virtually non-existent in China, in India and among primitive peoples. In part of course this is dietary. We eat too many processed foods and too much fat and sugar. We also tend to be too sedentary. But there is more to it than that. I believe it also has to do with the way we, as woman in the West, tend to deny our instinctual nature and, in doing so, we dis-empower our bodies – particularly in the area of the pelvis and thighs, the centre of sexual, procreative energies and the focus of cellulite development. Instead of being at ease in our flesh, we tend to put up with the body rather like some slightly cumbersome baggage we carry with us as we go about – to treat our bodies as objects.

# The Body As Energy

All thought, all feeling, every response to beauty and to horror is mediated through the body. In fact your body is the medium for experiencing everything in life. As any healthy 2 year old knows, when the body is fully alive you are fully alive. This aliveness is something women in the West often have to rediscover. In our society sexuality is written about, talked about and shown on screens everywhere yet it is frequently treated not from the point of view of instinct but intellectually, voyeuristically or mechanically. These attitudes, so implicit in our culture, tend to increase a woman's sense of distance from her own pelvis. Because mental and emotional attitudes (especially unconscious ones) strongly affect chemical and energetic states in the body, such a 'distancing' of oneself from the lower body can contribute to the development of static, dull areas – in other words cellulite.

Television, films and advertising don't help. They are replete with photographs of long-legged pencil-thin females who are meant to be paragons of womanhood and against whom we measure ourselves. Magazines and newspapers spend a large part of their time giving their readers advice about diets, clothes or exercise which supposedly will help us more closely approach whatever shape, size and texture body the general consensus considers ideal at any moment in time – all of which tends to make women feel bad about their bodies and distant from them. Meanwhile, millions of women, because of the way they are built, their personalities and their own values (whether or not these values operate consciously or unconsciously), have not a hope of ever looking like that ideal. And they suffer.

## The Dis-empowered Body

This suffering goes deep – far beyond the simple (yet often painful) feelings of inadequacy which come with having been built with broad shoulders, big feet or a flat chest when the world you live in tells you that you are *supposed* to be different. (Some of us alas have the misfortune of being blessed with all three.) For implicit in the whole way in which the body is presented in almost everything we do and think are two far more crippling assumptions: that the *body is separate from the spirit* or person and that it is ultimately *inferior*. These assumptions are anchored deep in the belief systems of the Greco-Roman and Christian traditions in which our society has developed. They have led us to view our bodies either as something not to be trusted – like a wild animal that needs taming lest it gets out of hand or like a physical object *outside* ourselves to be watched, studied and manipulated. All these attitudes tend to dis-empower women.

For most Western women their bodies are things separate from themselves, either to be prodded, criticized and hidden or narcissistically exposed as a sexual object – something to be used for gaining attention or drawing to oneself what one needs (or think one needs). In either case there is a sense of estrangement not only from the body but at a deeper level from oneself. Out of this estrangement comes a sense of powerlessness so that one begins to think that what one needs to be happy, to be complete, to be fulfilled can only be found *outside* oneself – by accomplishment in the world, or wearing the right clothes, by earning the love of a man or by conforming to some abstract ideal.

This sense of separateness from one's body creates the seedbed in which cellulite develops. In a very real way it uncentres body energy, drawing it away from the pelvis, thighs and belly where the seat of personal power lies. (The whole of martial-art training is designed to counteract this and to focus energy in the pelvic centre called the Hara.) So long as one is driven by a sense of separateness from one's body, whether you succeed or fail in getting what you want from the outside world is irrelevant. For neither success nor failure bring you any closer to living freely with real health and beauty and feeling good about yourself.

## Reclaiming The Body

Rediscovering the aliveness of the child and the innocence of bodily freedom can help heal the wounds of separation, and frees a woman to live in the fullness of her own being. Let the process begin with a real acceptance of your womanhood even if, for the moment, it is expressed in wide hips and fleshy thighs. Let your sexual energies in all their instinctual and irrational form *be* whatever they are instead of trying to fit them into some abstract idea of what they are *supposed* to be – whether that comes from your mind, or the mind of your mother, or the latest article on the subject in some woman's magazine. Treat your body lovingly and with respect – especially the lower part of your body. Such gentleness and respect will help you reclaim whatever energies in the pelvis and lower limbs which you may have been denying. This reclamation can help reconnect you with the deep ecology of sexuality. It is the most important connection you will ever make not only in freeing your body from the deadening presence of cellulite but also in feeding your creative life and keeping you well and young as the years pass.

# Making It Work

Getting it all together to bring about your own Cellulite Revolution is a lot easier than you might imagine. It demands only that you make a clear decision to do something for yourself and then that you keep whatever you need to hand – from a good skin brush to epsom salts, so it makes everything as easy as possible. The most important thing of all is your attitude towards yourself. You have got to feel that you really matter otherwise you will find yourself making excuses that you are either too 'busy' or too 'lazy' to bother. Care for your body and your body will repay you by becoming ever firmer, sleeker and smoother.

Here is an aide memoire.

## THE BREAKDOWN

- 2-3 day applefast.

- Skin brushing before bath or shower.

- 2-3 tablespoons of aloe vera on awakening, between lunch and dinner and just before bed.

- Epsom salts bath – 1–1½ cups of epsom salts in warm water for 20–30 minutes then go to bed or at least rest for 15 minutes.

## THE RECLAIM

- Conscientious food combining (see chart, page 77) which means separating concentrated proteins from concentrated starches.

- 1 teaspoon to 1 tablespoon of spirulina in juice or broth, 3 times a day.

- 2–3 tablets of Kervran's silica with breakfast.

- 3–6 capsules of Pro-Algin sea plants with breakfast.

- Seaweeds used in meals as often as you can.

- 15–60 minutes of aerobic exercise 3 to 5 times a week (and no more than 48 hours between each session).

- Skin brushing before a bath or shower.

- Massage with external anti-cellulite formula and special glove after bath or shower.

- Blitzguss (see page 62) at the end of each shower.

- Epsom salts bath when stressed or fatigued.

# Resources

**aloe vera and spirulina**: use only Lifestream brand from good health-food stores or ordered by post from: Lifestream Research UK, Ash House, Stedham, Midhurst, West Sussex GU29 0PT. Tel: 0730 813642. Fax: 0730 815109.

**epsom salts**: order household grade in 7lb bags from a chemist.

**good electrical massage glove**: Cellutherapie by Clairol – a vibromassage system complete with massage oil and smoothing lotion.

**good hand massage gloves and anti-cellulite cosmetics**: Elancyl do a good all-in-one treatment called MP24 complete with creams. Shiseido have an excellent lotion product in their Essential Energy range which comes in a special nobbily bottle that you use as a massage glove. Clarins do their own massage device which you can use together with their Multi-Actif Body Shaping Lotion. Decleor do excellent aromatherapy-based salon treatments as well as several good home use anti-cellulite products including Arome de Bain which you can put into the bath or massage onto the body after a bath or shower.

**good mineral waters**: both Volvic and Badoit are very pure and enhance digestion when taken with meals.

**herbal extracts of kola and fucus vesculosus**: by post from Gerard House Ltd, 736 Christchurch Road, Boscombe, Bournemouth, Dorset. Tel: 0202 434116.

**kervran's silica and pro-algin seaweed supplements**: by post from Health Innovations Ltd, Unit 10, Riverside Business Centre, Brighton Road, Shoreham, West Sussex BN43 6RE. Tel: 0273 440177. Fax: 0273 465325.

**marigold Swiss vegetable bouillon**: this instant broth powder based on vegetables and sea salt is available from health-food stores or direct from Marigold Foods, Unit 10, St Pancras Commercial Centre, 63 Pratt Street, London NW1 0BY. Tel: 071 267-7368. It comes in regular and low-salt forms. The low-salt form is excellent for making spirulina broth.

**rebounders**: mini-trampolines available from P.T. Leisure Ltd, New Rock House, Dymock, Glos. GL18 2BB. Tel: 0531 85888. Fax: 0531 85820.

**sea plants for cooking and salads**: can be bought from Japanese grocers or macrobiotic health shops.

**skin brush**: from good chemists – must have bristles of vegetable origin (not nylon).

# INDEX

Page numbers in **bold** type refer to major discussions